Bun.js in Action

Real-World Solutions for Building Modern Backends

Published by : Kumar.Abhiii

Copyright

Bun.js in Action: Real-World Solutions for Building Modern Backends

© 2024 Kumar.abhiii

All rights reserved.

No part of this publication may be reproduced, distributed, or transmitted in any form or by any means, including photocopying, recording, or other electronic or mechanical methods, without the prior written permission of the publisher, except in the case of brief quotations embodied in critical reviews and certain other non-commercial uses permitted by copyright law.

First Edition, 2024

Published by *Kumar Abhiii*

Dedication

To all the learners and the vibrant community,

Thank you for your endless support and inspiration. Your curiosity and passion for knowledge drive the future of technology. This book is dedicated to you.

Acknowledgments

I would like to express my heartfelt gratitude to everyone who supported me during the creation of this book. Special thanks to the Bun.js community and the developers behind this incredible tool, who continue to push the boundaries of web development.

I am also thankful for my friends and family, whose encouragement made this journey possible. Additionally, I want to acknowledge the vast resources available on the internet and the powerful AI tools that assisted me in crafting this book. Your contributions have made a significant impact.

Thank you all!

Preface

In recent years, Bun.js has rapidly gained traction as a high-performance JavaScript runtime, revolutionizing backend development. As someone passionate about modern backend technologies, I wanted to share my journey and knowledge of Bun.js to help developers take advantage of this powerful tool.

This book is designed for developers of all levels—from those just getting started with Bun.js to more advanced users looking to deepen their understanding. It focuses on real-world examples and practical applications, ensuring that you can implement the techniques and solutions in your own projects.

I hope this book inspires you to explore and build faster, more efficient backends using Bun.js.

Happy coding,
Kumar.abhiii

About the Author

Kumar.abhiii (Abhishek Kumar) is a passionate backend developer with extensive experience in modern web technologies. With a particular focus on JavaScript, TypeScript, and cutting-edge frameworks like Bun.js, he has helped build scalable, efficient backends for a wide range of applications.

In addition to his development work, Kumar.abhiii enjoys teaching and sharing his knowledge with the wider tech community. His goal is to simplify complex technologies and make them accessible to developers at all levels.

For more learning resources, visit: *https://9xcode.com/*

Table of Contents

Introduction to Bun.js..10
   Overview of Bun.js and Its Ecosystem...............................10
   Why Use Bun.js? Benefits and Key Features.....................11
   Setting Up Bun.js: Installation and Configuration..............12
   Running Your First Bun.js Project.......................................14
Getting Started with Bun.js and TypeScript.........................16
   Introduction to TypeScript in Bun.js...................................16
   Setting Up a TypeScript Project..17
   Understanding TypeScript Features in Bun.js...................19
   Type Safety and Development Best Practices...................21
Building HTTP Servers with Bun.js.......................................22
   Creating a Simple HTTP Server..22
   Handling Requests and Responses.....................................24
   Routing: Defining and Managing API Endpoints..............25
   Serving Static Files and Assets...27
Working with RESTful APIs in Bun.js....................................29
   Introduction to RESTful API Architecture.........................29
   Creating and Testing API Endpoints..................................31
   Handling HTTP Methods: GET, POST, PUT, DELETE.....33
   Building a Basic CRUD Application..................................36
Real-Time Applications with WebSockets..............................39
   Introduction to WebSockets and Real-Time Communication
....39
   Setting Up WebSocket Connections in Bun.js....................41
   Implementing Real-Time Features: Chat Application Example..43
   Managing WebSocket Connections and Data Streams........45
Working with Bun.js Workers...48
   Introduction to Bun.js Workers...48
   Offloading Tasks to Background Workers.........................50
   Practical Use Cases: Data Processing and Scheduling.......52
   Managing Worker Lifecycles and Performance.................54

- Advanced API Development...57
  - Middleware in Bun.js: Authentication and Logging...........57
  - Securing Your API: JWT, OAuth, and API Keys................60
  - Handling Errors and Validations in Bun.js APIs................63
  - API Versioning and Documentation....................................65
- Building Microservices with Bun.js...67
  - Introduction to Microservice Architecture..........................67
  - Decoupling Services: Designing Microservices with Bun.js 67
  - Communication Between Services: REST, WebSockets, and Message Queues..67
  - Managing and Scaling Microservices..................................68
- Database Integration and Data Persistence..............................69
  - Connecting Bun.js to Databases (SQL and NoSQL)..........69
  - Setting Up a Database with Bun.js (e.g., PostgreSQL, MongoDB)..71
  - Implementing ORM with Bun.js: Working with Prisma/TypeORM..72
  - Database Transactions and Best Practices..........................74
- Deploying Bun.js Applications...75
  - Preparing Bun.js Applications for Production....................75
  - Deploying on Cloud Platforms (e.g., Vercel, AWS, DigitalOcean)...76
  - Managing Environment Variables and Configurations.......77
  - Monitoring and Performance Optimization........................78
- Testing and Debugging Bun.js Applications............................79
  - Writing Unit and Integration Tests.....................................79
  - Using Bun.js Testing Tools (e.g., Bun's Built-in Test Runner)..81
  - Debugging Techniques and Tools for Bun.js......................82
  - Ensuring Performance with Load Testing..........................83
- Conclusion and Next Steps...84
  - Recap of Key Bun.js Concepts..84
  - Best Practices for Bun.js Development...............................85
  - Resources for Continued Learning (Documentation, Communities, Projects)..86
  - Looking Forward: The Future of Bun.js.............................87
- Thank You and Congratulations!..88

Bun.js in Action

Introduction to Bun.js

Overview of Bun.js and Its Ecosystem

Bun.js is a modern, ultra-fast JavaScript runtime designed to improve the performance and developer experience of building backend applications. Unlike Node.js or Deno, Bun.js aims to be faster at executing JavaScript, managing HTTP servers, and running tasks that typically require heavy computational resources. Built from the ground up with speed and simplicity in mind, Bun.js is perfect for creating high-performance APIs, microservices, and real-time applications.

Key Components of the Bun.js Ecosystem:

- **JavaScript/TypeScript Support**: Seamlessly integrates both JavaScript and TypeScript.
- **HTTP Server**: Bun.js has an extremely fast HTTP server built-in, making it ideal for API development.
- **Built-in Bundler**: Automatically bundles your JavaScript/TypeScript files for production.
- **Package Manager**: Bun.js has its own package manager, offering faster dependency management compared to npm or yarn.
- **Test Runner**: Bun.js comes with a built-in test runner for unit testing without needing additional tools.

Why Use Bun.js? Benefits and Key Features

Bun.js is gaining popularity for a variety of reasons, especially in the backend development world. Here's why:

- **Speed**: Bun.js is designed for speed. It handles HTTP requests, runs JavaScript, and manages dependencies much faster than Node.js.
- **Performance**: Lower memory usage and faster execution time make Bun.js ideal for high-performance applications.
- **Native TypeScript Support**: Write modern, type-safe JavaScript using TypeScript without extra configuration.
- **Built-in Tooling**: With a built-in bundler, test runner, and package manager, Bun.js eliminates the need for multiple external tools, simplifying the development workflow.
- **Compatibility**: Bun.js is compatible with Node.js APIs, which makes transitioning or sharing code across platforms easier.

In short, Bun.js optimizes every part of the development and execution process, making backend development quicker and more efficient.

Setting Up Bun.js: Installation and Configuration

Step 1: Installing Bun.js

To get started with Bun.js, you first need to install it on your machine. Here's how you can install Bun.js using your terminal:

```
curl https://bun.sh/install | bash
```

This command will download and install Bun.js. After installation, you can verify the installation by running the following command:

```
bun -version
```

If the version number is displayed, you're good to go!

Step 2: Configuring Bun.js

Once installed, Bun.js is ready to use with minimal configuration. By default, Bun.js will handle your JavaScript and TypeScript projects efficiently. However, you can create a configuration file to customize how Bun.js behaves:

```
bun init
```

This command will create a **bunfig.json** file where you can define custom settings for bundling, dependency management, or file handling.

Running Your First Bun.js Project

Now that Bun.js is installed, let's run a simple project to get a feel for how fast it is.

Step 1: Create a Simple HTTP Server

Create a new file called **server.ts** and add the following code:

```typescript
import { serve } from "bun";
serve({
  port: 3000,
  fetch(request) {
    return new Response("Hello, Bun.js!");
  },
});
```

This simple script creates an HTTP server that listens on port 3000 and responds with "Hello, Bun.js!" to every request.

Step 2: Running the Server

To run the server, open your terminal and type:

```
bun run server.ts
```

Once the server is running, open your browser and navigate to `http://localhost:3000`. You should see the message **"Hello, Bun.js!"** displayed.

Congratulations! You've just built and run your first Bun.js project. This small example demonstrates how easy and fast it is to get started with Bun.js.

Getting Started with Bun.js and TypeScript

Introduction to TypeScript in Bun.js

TypeScript is a superset of JavaScript that adds static types, enabling developers to catch errors at compile time rather than runtime. Bun.js fully supports TypeScript, making it an excellent choice for building scalable and maintainable applications. With TypeScript, you can leverage features like interfaces, enums, and generics, enhancing your code's robustness and clarity.

Using TypeScript in your Bun.js projects allows for better collaboration, as team members can understand the data structures and types in use without delving deep into the implementation details. This can significantly improve developer productivity and reduce the likelihood of bugs.

Setting Up a TypeScript Project

To set up a Bun.js project with TypeScript, follow these steps:

Step 1: Create a New Project Directory

First, create a new directory for your project:

```
mkdir my-bun-ts-project
cd my-bun-ts-project
```

Step 2: Initialize Your Bun.js Project

Next, initialize your Bun.js project:

```
bun init
```

This command will generate a **bunfig.json** file and create a basic project structure.

Step 3: Install TypeScript

Now, install TypeScript as a development dependency:

```
bun add typescript --dev
```

Step 4: Create a TypeScript Configuration File

Create a **tsconfig.json** file in the root of your project:

```
{
  "compilerOptions": {
    "target": "ESNext",
    "module": "ESNext",
    "strict": true,
    "esModuleInterop": true,
    "skipLibCheck": true,
    "forceConsistentCasingInFileNames": true
  },
  "include": ["src/**/*.ts"]
}
```

This configuration enables strict type-checking and sets the target to the latest ECMAScript version, ensuring compatibility with Bun.js.

Step 5: Create Your First TypeScript File

Create a new directory called **src**, and inside it, create a file named **index.ts**:

```
const greet = (name: string): string => {
  return `Hello, ${name}! Welcome to Bun.js with TypeScript.`;
};

console.log(greet("Developer"));
```

Understanding TypeScript Features in Bun.js

Bun.js allows you to harness various TypeScript features seamlessly. Here are some essential features you should consider:

- **Static Typing**: TypeScript allows you to define the type of variables, function parameters, and return values. This reduces runtime errors and improves code readability.

```
let age: number = 30;
```

- **Interfaces**: Use interfaces to define the shape of an object. This is particularly useful for API responses or complex data structures.

```
interface User {
  id: number;
  name: string;
  email: string;
}

const user: User = {
  id: 1,
  name: "Alice",
  email: "alice@example.com",
};
```

- **Enums**: Enums provide a way to define named constants, improving code clarity.

```
enum Status {
  Active,
  Inactive,
  Pending,
}

const currentUserStatus: Status = Status.Active;
```

- **Generics**: Generics allow you to create reusable components that work with various types.

```
function identity<T>(arg: T): T {
  return arg;
}

const output = identity<string>("Hello, Bun.js!");
```

Type Safety and Development Best Practices

1. **Enable Strict Mode**: Always enable strict mode in your **tsconfig.json**. This ensures you are catching potential errors early in the development process.

2. **Use Meaningful Types**: Define clear and descriptive types for your variables and function parameters. This enhances code readability and maintainability.

3. **Type Annotations**: Use type annotations wherever possible to provide clarity on what types are expected.

4. **Utilize Interfaces**: When dealing with complex data structures, leverage interfaces to define clear contracts within your code.

5. **Error Handling**: Always handle errors gracefully, particularly when dealing with external APIs or databases. TypeScript's type system can help you manage expected error types.

6. **Keep Dependencies Up to Date**: Regularly update your dependencies to ensure you are using the latest features and security patches.

Building HTTP Servers with Bun.js

Creating a Simple HTTP Server

Bun.js makes it incredibly easy to build fast HTTP servers thanks to its built-in support for serving web requests. Let's start by creating a simple HTTP server.

Create a file named **server.ts** with the following code:

```typescript
import { serve } from "bun";

serve({
  port: 3000,
  fetch(request) {
    return new Response("Hello, Bun.js!");
  },
});
```

In this example:

- **serve**: The `serve` function starts an HTTP server.
- **port**: Defines the port the server will listen on (in this case, 3000).
- **fetch(request)**: This function handles every incoming request and returns a response. Here, we respond with "Hello, Bun.js!" to every request.

To run the server, use the following command:

```
bun run server.ts
```

Open your browser and go to **http://localhost:3000**, and you'll see the message **"Hello, Bun.js!"** displayed.

Handling Requests and Responses

Handling HTTP requests and sending responses is straightforward with Bun.js. The `fetch` function receives a **Request** object, which contains information about the incoming HTTP request, such as headers, body, and method. You can respond by returning a **Response** object.

Let's expand on the previous example by inspecting request details and sending more dynamic responses:

```
import { serve } from "bun";

serve({
  port: 3000,
  fetch(request) {
    const { method, url } = request;
    return new Response(`Request received! Method: ${method}, URL: ${url}`);
  },
});
```

In this example:

- **method**: Retrieves the HTTP method used (e.g., GET, POST).
- **url**: Fetches the requested URL path.

This will dynamically return the HTTP method and URL for each request made to the server.

Routing: Defining and Managing API Endpoints

In most real-world applications, you need to define multiple API endpoints to handle different types of requests. Bun.js doesn't come with built-in routing out of the box, but you can easily implement basic routing logic.

Here's an example of how to handle different routes:

```
import { serve } from "bun";
serve({
  port: 3000,
  fetch(request) {
    const url = new URL(request.url);

    if (url.pathname === "/") {
      return new Response("Welcome to the Bun.js homepage!");
    } else if (url.pathname === "/about") {
      return new Response("This is the About page.");
    } else {
      return new Response("Page not found", { status: 404 });
    }
  },
});
```

In this example:

- **URL parsing**: We use the **URL** constructor to parse the request **URL** and extract the pathname (e.g., **/, /about**).
- **Custom responses**: Depending on the route, the server returns different content. If the requested route doesn't exist, we return a 404 error.

You can extend this routing logic to handle more complex paths, query parameters, or even integrate with a router library.

Serving Static Files and Assets

Bun.js can also be used to serve static files like HTML, CSS, and JavaScript, which is common in web applications. Let's see how to serve static files like a simple HTML page.

First, create a folder structure like this:

```
/my-bun-server
 ├── public/
 │   └── index.html
 └── server.ts
```

In the **public/index.html** file, add the following HTML code:

```
<!DOCTYPE html>
<html lang="en">
<head>
  <meta charset="UTF-8">
  <meta name="viewport" content="width=device-width, initial-scale=1.0">
  <title>Bun.js Server</title>
</head>
<body>
  <h1>Hello, this is a static page served by Bun.js!</h1>
</body>
</html>
```

Now, update the **server.ts** file to serve the static HTML file:

```
import { serve } from "bun";
import { file } from "bun";

serve({
  port: 3000,
  fetch(request) {
    const url = new URL(request.url);

    if (url.pathname === "/") {
      return new
Response(file("public/index.html"));
    } else {
      return new Response("File not found",
{ status: 404 });
    }
  },
});
```

In this example:

- **file()**: The **file** function reads the content of the specified file and serves it as the response.
- **Static file serving**: If the request URL matches /, the server returns the **index.html** file from the `public` directory.

Visit **http://localhost:3000**, and you'll see the HTML page rendered in your browser. This shows how Bun.js can be used to serve static assets.

Working with RESTful APIs in Bun.js

Introduction to RESTful API Architecture

REST (Representational State Transfer) is an architectural style commonly used for building APIs. It relies on stateless communication and uses standard HTTP methods like GET, POST, PUT, and DELETE to manage resources. Each API endpoint in a RESTful architecture corresponds to a specific resource, and these endpoints provide a clean way to interact with data or services.

Key Principles of RESTful APIs:

- **Stateless**: Every HTTP request from a client to a server must contain all the necessary information for the server to fulfill the request. The server doesn't retain client state between requests.
- **Uniform Interface**: Resources are identified through unique URIs, and standard HTTP methods are used to perform actions on them.
- **Resource Representation**: Resources are typically represented in JSON format, making it easy to exchange data between systems.

- **HTTP Methods**: REST APIs rely on well-defined HTTP methods to manage resources:
    - **GET**: Retrieve data from the server.
    - **POST**: Send new data to the server.
    - **PUT**: Update existing data.
    - **DELETE**: Remove data.

Creating and Testing API Endpoints

Let's start by creating some simple API endpoints using Bun.js. First, create a file called **api.ts**:

```
import { serve } from "bun";

serve({
  port: 3000,
  fetch(request) {
    const url = new URL(request.url);

    if (url.pathname === "/api/greet" && request.method === "GET") {
        const name = url.searchParams.get("name") || "Guest";
        return new Response(JSON.stringify({ message: `Hello, ${name}!` }), {
          headers: { "Content-Type": "application/json" },
        });
    }

    return new Response("Not Found", { status: 404 });
  },
});
```

In this example:

- **API Endpoint**: We define an endpoint **/api/greet** that takes a **name** parameter from the query string.

- **GET Request**: This endpoint only responds to **GET** requests. If no name is provided, it defaults to "Guest."
- **JSON Response**: The server responds with a **JSON** object that contains a greeting message.

To test this API, run the server:

```
bun run api.ts
```

Open your browser or a tool like Postman, and try accessing the endpoint:

```
http://localhost:3000/api/greet?name=Abhiii
```

You should receive a response like:

```
{
  "message": "Hello, Abhiii!"
}
```

Handling HTTP Methods: GET, POST, PUT, DELETE

In a RESTful API, different HTTP methods are used to interact with resources. Let's see how to handle common HTTP methods in Bun.js: GET, POST, PUT, and DELETE.

Update your `api.ts` file as follows:

```
import { serve } from "bun";

let data: { id: number; name: string }[] = [
  { id: 1, name: "Alice" },
  { id: 2, name: "Bob" },
];

serve({
  port: 3000,
  fetch(request) {
    const url = new URL(request.url);

    // Handle GET requests
    if (url.pathname === "/api/users" && request.method === "GET") {
        return new Response(JSON.stringify(data), {
          headers: { "Content-Type": "application/json" },
        });
    }

    // Handle POST requests (add new user)
    if (url.pathname === "/api/users" && request.method === "POST") {
        const newUser = { id: data.length + 1, name: "New User" }; // Simplified example
```

```js
      data.push(newUser);
      return new
Response(JSON.stringify(newUser), {
        status: 201,
        headers: { "Content-Type":
"application/json" },
      });
    }

    // Handle PUT requests (update user)
    if
(url.pathname.startsWith("/api/users/") &&
request.method === "PUT") {
      const id =
parseInt(url.pathname.split("/").pop() ||
"");
      const user = data.find(u => u.id ===
id);
      if (user) {
        user.name = "Updated User";
        return new
Response(JSON.stringify(user), {
          headers: { "Content-Type":
"application/json" },
        });
      }
      return new Response("User not found",
{ status: 404 });
    }

    // Handle DELETE requests (delete user)
    if
(url.pathname.startsWith("/api/users/") &&
request.method === "DELETE") {
      const id =
parseInt(url.pathname.split("/").pop() ||
"");
      data = data.filter(u => u.id !== id);
      return new Response("User deleted",
{ status: 204 });
```

```
    }

    return new Response("Not Found",
{ status: 404 });
  },
});
```

Here's what this code does:

- **GET /api/users**: Returns a list of all users.
- **POST /api/users**: Adds a new user (simplified with default data).
- **PUT /api/users/**
  : Updates the user's name by ID.
- **DELETE /api/users/**
  : Deletes the user with the specified ID.

Each endpoint responds with JSON and uses the appropriate HTTP method.

Building a Basic CRUD Application

Now that you've seen how to handle the main HTTP methods, let's combine everything into a basic **CRUD (Create, Read, Update, Delete)** API for managing a list of users.

We'll continue using the `data` array to simulate a database, and we'll handle each operation using the respective HTTP methods:

- **Create (POST)**: Add a new user to the list.
- **Read (GET)**: Retrieve all users or a single user by ID.
- **Update (PUT)**: Modify an existing user's data.
- **Delete (DELETE)**: Remove a user from the list.

Here's the complete code for a basic CRUD API:

```
import { serve } from "bun";

let data: { id: number; name: string }[] = [
  { id: 1, name: "Alice" },
  { id: 2, name: "Bob" },
];

serve({
  port: 3000,
  fetch(request) {
    const url = new URL(request.url);

    // GET: Fetch all users
    if (url.pathname === "/api/users" && request.method === "GET") {
```

```js
        return new 
Response(JSON.stringify(data), { 
        headers: { "Content-Type": 
"application/json" }, 
      }); 
    } 

    // POST: Add a new user 
    if (url.pathname === "/api/users" && 
request.method === "POST") { 
      const newUser = { id: data.length + 1, 
name: "New User" }; 
      data.push(newUser); 
      return new 
Response(JSON.stringify(newUser), { 
        status: 201, 
        headers: { "Content-Type": 
"application/json" }, 
      }); 
    } 

    // PUT: Update a user by ID 
    if 
(url.pathname.startsWith("/api/users/") && 
request.method === "PUT") { 
      const id = 
parseInt(url.pathname.split("/").pop() || 
""); 
      const user = data.find(u => u.id === 
id); 
      if (user) { 
        user.name = "Updated User"; 
        return new 
Response(JSON.stringify(user), { 
          headers: { "Content-Type": 
"application/json" }, 
        }); 
      } 
      return new Response("User not found", 
{ status: 404 }); 
```

```
    }

    // DELETE: Remove a user by ID
    if
(url.pathname.startsWith("/api/users/") &&
request.method === "DELETE") {
        const id =
parseInt(url.pathname.split("/").pop() ||
"");
        data = data.filter(u => u.id !== id);
        return new Response("User deleted",
{ status: 204 });
    }

    return new Response("Not Found",
{ status: 404 });
  },
});
```

With this code, you've built a complete CRUD API that can:

- **Create** new users
- **Read** existing users
- **Update** users by ID
- **Delete** users by ID

This provides a solid foundation for building more advanced RESTful APIs using Bun.js.

Real-Time Applications with WebSockets

Introduction to WebSockets and Real-Time Communication

WebSockets enable two-way communication between a client and server over a single, long-lived connection. Unlike traditional HTTP requests, which are stateless and involve frequent re-establishment of connections, WebSockets allow for continuous, real-time data exchange, making them ideal for applications like chat systems, live updates, and multiplayer games.

Benefits of WebSockets:

- **Low Latency**: Once the connection is established, messages can be exchanged instantly.
- **Bidirectional Communication**: Both the server and client can send messages independently at any time.
- **Persistent Connection**: After the initial handshake, the connection remains open, reducing overhead compared to repetitive HTTP requests.

Common real-time applications using WebSockets include:

- Live chat systems
- Real-time data dashboards
- Multiplayer games
- Collaboration tools (e.g., Google Docs)

Setting Up WebSocket Connections in Bun.js

Bun.js has excellent support for WebSockets, making it easy to build real-time applications. Let's start by setting up a simple WebSocket server.

Create a file called **websocket.ts**:

```typescript
import { WebSocketServer } from "bun";

const wss = new WebSocketServer({ port: 8080 });

wss.on("connection", (ws) => {
  console.log("New client connected");

  // Send a welcome message to the client
  ws.send("Welcome to the WebSocket server!");

  // Handle incoming messages from the client
  ws.on("message", (message) => {
    console.log("Received message:", message);
    ws.send(`Echo: ${message}`);
  });

  // Handle connection close
  ws.on("close", () => {
    console.log("Client disconnected");
  });
});
```

```
console.log("WebSocket server is running on
ws://localhost:8080");
```

In this example:

- **WebSocketServer**: The `WebSocketServer` class is used to create a new WebSocket server that listens on port 8080.
- **connection event**: When a new client connects, the `on("connection")` handler is triggered, allowing communication with the client.
- **message event**: When a message is received from the client, the server responds by echoing the message back.
- **close event**: The `close` event is triggered when a client disconnects.

To test the WebSocket server, use a WebSocket client in your browser's developer tools or an application like websocat.

Implementing Real-Time Features: Chat Application Example

To demonstrate the power of WebSockets, let's build a simple real-time chat application where multiple clients can connect and exchange messages.

Update your **websocket.ts** file as follows:

```
import { WebSocketServer } from "bun";

const wss = new WebSocketServer({ port: 8080 });

wss.on("connection", (ws) => {
  console.log("A new user has connected");

  ws.send("Welcome to the chat!");

  // Broadcast incoming messages to all connected clients
  ws.on("message", (message) => {
    console.log("Broadcasting message:", message);
    wss.clients.forEach((client) => {
      if (client.readyState === ws.OPEN) {
        client.send(message);
      }
    });
  });

  // Handle client disconnection
  ws.on("close", () => {
    console.log("A user has disconnected");
  });
});
```

```
console.log("Chat WebSocket server is
running on ws://localhost:8080");
```

In this example:

- **Broadcasting messages**: When one client sends a message, it is broadcast to all connected clients using the **wss.clients.forEach()** loop.
- **Handling multiple clients**: The server can handle multiple WebSocket connections simultaneously, allowing all clients to participate in the chat.

To test the chat application, open multiple browser tabs and connect them to **ws://localhost:8080**. When one client sends a message, all connected clients will receive it in real time.

Managing WebSocket Connections and Data Streams

Managing WebSocket connections efficiently is crucial for real-time applications. Here are a few tips and best practices:

1. Handling Connection Limits

If your application scales, you'll need to handle a large number of WebSocket connections. You can manage connection limits by checking the number of active clients and rejecting connections once a limit is reached.

```
const MAX_CONNECTIONS = 100;
let activeConnections = 0;

wss.on("connection", (ws) => {
  if (activeConnections >= MAX_CONNECTIONS)
  {
     ws.send("Connection limit reached");
     ws.close();
     return;
  }
  activeConnections++;

  ws.on("close", () => {
    activeConnections--;
  });
});
```

2. Heartbeats and Connection Monitoring

To ensure that the WebSocket connections remain active and healthy, you can implement a heartbeat mechanism. This helps detect broken connections:

```
setInterval(() => {
  wss.clients.forEach((client) => {
    if (client.isAlive === false) return
client.terminate();
    client.isAlive = false;
    client.ping();
  });
}, 30000);   // Send a heartbeat every 30 seconds

wss.on("pong", () => {
  client.isAlive = true;
});
```

This example ensures that the server checks whether each client is responsive and terminates any inactive connections.

3. Streaming Data in Real-Time

In addition to handling user messages, WebSockets can be used for real-time data streaming. For example, you can stream real-time stock prices, live game scores, or sensor data from IoT devices:

```
setInterval(() => {
  const data = { stockPrice:
getLatestStockPrice() };
  wss.clients.forEach((client) => {
    if (client.readyState === ws.OPEN) {
      client.send(JSON.stringify(data));
    }
  });
}, 1000);  // Send stock price updates every second
```

In this case, the server broadcasts live stock prices to all connected clients every second, simulating a real-time data stream.

Working with Bun.js Workers

Introduction to Bun.js Workers

Bun.js Workers allow you to run JavaScript code in the background, separate from the main thread of your application. This is particularly useful for offloading CPU-intensive or time-consuming tasks that could block the main event loop, ensuring that your server can continue handling requests efficiently.

Workers in Bun.js are similar to web workers in browser environments, and they provide a simple yet powerful API for managing background tasks.

Why use Workers?

- **Parallelism**: Workers run in parallel with the main thread, enabling you to handle multiple tasks concurrently.
- **Non-blocking**: Long-running tasks can be offloaded to workers, preventing the main server from becoming unresponsive.

- **Performance**: By using workers, you can improve your application's performance by distributing workloads across different threads.

Offloading Tasks to Background Workers

To get started with workers in Bun.js, let's look at how to create a worker and offload tasks.

Create a new file called **worker.js** for the worker code:

```js
self.onmessage = function (event) {
  const data = event.data;
  // Simulate a heavy task, e.g., processing data
  const result = data * 2; // Example task: double the number
  self.postMessage(result); // Send result back to the main thread
};
```

In this simple worker, the **onmessage** handler listens for messages from the main thread. The worker receives data, processes it, and sends the result back using **postMessage.**

Next, create the main server file, **server.ts**:

```ts
import { Worker } from "bun";

// Create a worker and offload a task
const worker = new Worker("./worker.js");

worker.onmessage = (event) => {
  console.log("Result from worker:", event.data);
};
```

```
worker.postMessage(10); // Send a task to
the worker
```

In this example:

- **Worker**: A new worker is created using the `Worker` constructor, pointing to the **worker.js** file.
- **postMessage**: The main thread sends a task (in this case, the number `10`) to the worker using `postMessage`.
- **onmessage**: The main thread listens for messages from the worker and logs the result.

With this setup, the main thread remains free to handle incoming HTTP requests or other tasks while the worker processes the background task in parallel.

Practical Use Cases: Data Processing and Scheduling

Workers can be used for various real-world scenarios where background tasks are needed. Here are two common use cases:

1. Data Processing

In applications that require intensive data processing, such as generating reports, image processing, or encrypting data, workers can handle these tasks efficiently without slowing down the main thread.

For example, processing large amounts of data in the background:

```
self.onmessage = function (event) {
  const data = event.data;
  const processedData = data.map(item => item * 2); // Example: double each number in the array
  self.postMessage(processedData);
};
```

The main thread sends an array of numbers to the worker, which processes the data (e.g., by doubling each number) and returns the result.

2. Task Scheduling

You can also use workers for scheduling tasks that need to run periodically or at specific intervals, such as sending notifications, generating periodic reports, or performing routine cleanups.

Here's an example of using a worker for periodic task scheduling:

```
self.onmessage = function () {
  setInterval(() => {
    const timestamp = new Date().toISOString();
    self.postMessage(`Task executed at ${timestamp}`);
  }, 5000); // Execute task every 5 seconds
};
```

The worker periodically executes the task and sends updates back to the main thread, which can handle scheduling without blocking the main event loop.

Managing Worker Lifecycles and Performance

When working with workers, it's important to manage their lifecycles and ensure they perform optimally. Here are a few best practices:

1. Worker Creation and Termination

Workers are independent of the main thread and need to be explicitly terminated when they are no longer needed. This helps avoid memory leaks or unnecessary resource usage.

```
const worker = new Worker("./worker.js");

// Terminate the worker when the task is complete
worker.onmessage = (event) => {
  console.log("Worker finished:", event.data);
  worker.terminate();
};
```

In this example, the worker is terminated after completing its task to free up system resources.

2. Task Batching for Efficiency

Rather than creating multiple workers for individual tasks, you can batch similar tasks together and process them in a single worker instance. This reduces the overhead of managing multiple workers.

```
self.onmessage = function (event) {
  const tasks = event.data;
  const results = tasks.map(task => task * 2);
  self.postMessage(results);
};
```

The worker processes an array of tasks in one go and returns the results.

3. Monitoring Worker Performance

Workers can handle heavy tasks, but it's essential to monitor their performance, especially in production environments. Monitoring tools or logging mechanisms can help track worker performance and ensure tasks are completed within the expected time frames.

Here's an example of logging worker performance:

```
const worker = new Worker("./worker.js");
const startTime = Date.now();

worker.onmessage = (event) => {
  const duration = Date.now() - startTime;
  console.log(`Worker completed task in ${duration} ms`);
  worker.terminate();
};
```

In this case, the time taken by the worker to complete the task is logged, giving you insight into performance metrics.

Advanced API Development

Middleware in Bun.js: Authentication and Logging

Middleware in Bun.js acts as a layer between the server and the API endpoints, allowing you to process requests, validate data, and add features like authentication, logging, and error handling. Middleware functions are essential for building scalable and secure applications.

Authentication Middleware

A common use of middleware is handling authentication. You can implement authentication in Bun.js using JSON Web Tokens (JWT), API keys, or OAuth. Below is an example of a JWT-based authentication middleware:

```
import { verify } from "jsonwebtoken";

const authMiddleware = (req, res, next) => {
  const token = req.headers.authorization?.split(" ")[1];

  if (!token) {
    return res.status(401).json({ message: "Unauthorized" });
  }
```

```
  try {
    const decoded = verify(token,
process.env.JWT_SECRET);
    req.user = decoded;
    next(); // Proceed to the next
middleware or route handler
  } catch (error) {
    return res.status(403).json({ message:
"Forbidden" });
  }
};

// Example usage with an endpoint
app.use(authMiddleware);
app.get("/protected", (req, res) => {
  res.json({ message: "This is a protected
route", user: req.user });
});
```

In this example:

- **verify**: The `verify` function checks if the JWT token is valid and decodes it.
- **next()**: The `next` function is called to proceed to the next route handler if the user is authenticated.

Logging Middleware

Logging is another key use of middleware, helping you track requests, errors, and performance metrics.

Here's a simple logging middleware:

```
const loggerMiddleware = (req, res, next) =>
{
  console.log(`[${new Date().toISOString()}] ${req.method} ${req.url}`);
  next(); // Move to the next middleware or route handler
};

app.use(loggerMiddleware);
```

This middleware logs the HTTP method and URL of incoming requests, along with the timestamp. It's helpful for monitoring and debugging API requests.

Securing Your API: JWT, OAuth, and API Keys

Securing APIs is crucial to protect sensitive data and ensure that only authorized users can access certain endpoints. Here are common techniques for securing your Bun.js APIs:

1. JSON Web Tokens (JWT)

JWTs are widely used for API authentication. They encode user information into a token, which is then included in API requests.

Here's how you can generate and validate a JWT in Bun.js:

```
import { sign } from "jsonwebtoken";

// Generating a JWT
const generateToken = (user) => {
  return sign({ id: user.id, email: user.email }, process.env.JWT_SECRET, {
    expiresIn: "1h",
  });
};

// Example usage
const token = generateToken({ id: 1, email: "user@example.com" });
```

2. OAuth

OAuth is a widely used framework for token-based authentication. It allows third-party applications to access a user's resources without exposing their credentials.

Bun.js can integrate with OAuth providers like Google, GitHub, or Facebook by using libraries such as `passport.js`. For example:

```
import passport from "passport";
import { Strategy as GoogleStrategy } from "passport-google-oauth20";

passport.use(new GoogleStrategy({
   clientID: process.env.GOOGLE_CLIENT_ID,
   clientSecret: process.env.GOOGLE_CLIENT_SECRET,
   callbackURL: "/auth/google/callback"
}, (token, tokenSecret, profile, done) => {
   // Find or create user in database
   return done(null, profile);
}));

app.get("/auth/google",
passport.authenticate("google", { scope: ["profile", "email"] }));
```

3. API Keys

API keys provide a simple mechanism for authenticating users or applications accessing your API. You can check for an API key in the request headers or query parameters.

Example API key validation middleware:

```
const apiKeyMiddleware = (req, res, next) => {
  const apiKey = req.headers["x-api-key"];
  if (apiKey !== process.env.API_KEY) {
    return res.status(401).json({ message: "Invalid API key" });
  }
  next();
};

app.use(apiKeyMiddleware);
```

Handling Errors and Validations in Bun.js APIs

Error handling and validation are critical to ensuring the reliability and user-friendliness of your APIs.

Error Handling

Bun.js allows you to create custom error-handling middleware to catch errors and provide meaningful responses. Here's an example of centralized error handling:

```
const errorHandler = (err, req, res, next)
=> {
  console.error(err.stack);
  res.status(500).json({ message: "An error occurred", error: err.message });
};

// Example usage
app.use(errorHandler);
```

This middleware catches any unhandled errors in the API and returns a consistent error response with a `500` status code.

Request Validation

Request validation ensures that API consumers send the correct data format and types. You can use libraries like `joi` or implement your own validation middleware.

Here's an example of using `joi` for request validation:

```
import Joi from "joi";

const userSchema = Joi.object({
  name: Joi.string().min(3).required(),
  email: Joi.string().email().required(),
});

const validateUser = (req, res, next) => {
  const { error } = userSchema.validate(req.body);
  if (error) {
    return res.status(400).json({ message: error.details[0].message });
  }
  next();
};

// Example usage
app.post("/users", validateUser, (req, res) => {
  res.json({ message: "User is valid!" });
});
```

In this example:

- The **validateUser** middleware validates the incoming request body based on the defined schema and returns an error response if the data is invalid.

API Versioning and Documentation

As your API evolves, it's essential to manage versions and provide clear documentation for users. Versioning allows you to introduce new features or breaking changes without affecting existing users.

API Versioning

You can implement versioning by including the version number in your API endpoints:

```
app.get("/v1/users", (req, res) => {
  res.json({ message: "Version 1 API" });
});

app.get("/v2/users", (req, res) => {
  res.json({ message: "Version 2 API with new features" });
});
```

Alternatively, versioning can be handled through request headers or query parameters.

API Documentation

Proper documentation helps developers understand how to interact with your API. Tools like **Swagger** or **Postman** can generate interactive API documentation.

To add Swagger to your Bun.js API, you can use the **swagger-ui-express** package:

```
import swaggerUi from "swagger-ui-express";
import swaggerDocument from
"./swagger.json";

app.use("/api-docs", swaggerUi.serve,
swaggerUi.setup(swaggerDocument));
```

With this setup, users can visit **/api-docs** to view and interact with your API documentation.

Building Microservices with Bun.js

Introduction to Microservice Architecture

Microservices break down applications into smaller, independent services that handle specific functions. This architecture allows for easier scaling, development, and deployment.

Decoupling Services: Designing Microservices with Bun.js

Each microservice in Bun.js is self-contained, focusing on a single business function. You can organize services by domain, such as user management, billing, or notifications. Using Bun.js, you can deploy lightweight, efficient microservices that communicate over APIs.

Communication Between Services: REST, WebSockets, and Message Queues

Microservices can communicate through various protocols:

- **REST**: Ideal for synchronous HTTP requests between services.
- **WebSockets**: Used for real-time communication, like notifications or chat systems.

- **Message Queues**: Asynchronous messaging, enabling services to interact without waiting for a response.

Managing and Scaling Microservices

To scale microservices, you can run multiple instances and distribute load using tools like **Docker** and **Kubernetes**. Bun.js, with its fast performance, ensures that even when scaling, the services remain lightweight and efficient.

Database Integration and Data Persistence

Connecting Bun.js to Databases (SQL and NoSQL)

Bun.js supports integration with both SQL (e.g., PostgreSQL, MySQL) and NoSQL (e.g., MongoDB) databases, enabling flexible data storage solutions. You can use libraries like pg for PostgreSQL or mongoose for MongoDB to establish connections and execute queries.

For example, connecting to PostgreSQL:

```
import { Client } from "pg";

const client = new Client({
  connectionString: process.env.DATABASE_URL,
});

await client.connect();
```

For MongoDB:

```
import { connect } from "mongoose";
```

```
await connect(process.env.MONGODB_URI);
```

Setting Up a Database with Bun.js (e.g., PostgreSQL, MongoDB)

To set up a database, you'll first need to configure your environment variables and create the database instance. In the case of PostgreSQL, you can use **pgAdmin** or the PostgreSQL CLI to create databases and manage users.

For MongoDB, you can use **MongoDB Atlas** to set up cloud-hosted databases or run MongoDB locally using Docker. Once the database is running, Bun.js can connect to it using the appropriate database drivers.

Implementing ORM with Bun.js: Working with Prisma/TypeORM

Object-Relational Mapping (ORM) tools simplify database interactions by allowing you to work with models instead of writing raw SQL queries. With Bun.js, you can use popular ORMs like **Prisma** or **TypeORM** for structured data management.

Example using Prisma:

- Install Prisma and initialize it in your project:

```
npm install prisma
npx prisma init
```

- Define a schema in `prisma/schema.prisma`:

```
model User {
  id    Int     @id @default(autoincrement())
  name  String
  email String  @unique
}
```

- Use the Prisma client in Bun.js to interact with the database:

```
import { PrismaClient } from
'@prisma/client';
const prisma = new PrismaClient();

const users = await prisma.user.findMany();
console.log(users);
```

Database Transactions and Best Practices

Transactions ensure consistency by grouping multiple database operations into a single unit. If any operation fails, the entire transaction is rolled back, ensuring no partial changes are saved.

Here's an example of using transactions in Bun.js with PostgreSQL:

```
await client.query('BEGIN');
try {
  await client.query('INSERT INTO users (name) VALUES ($1)', ['John']);
  await client.query('UPDATE accounts SET balance = balance - 100 WHERE id = $1', [userId]);
  await client.query('COMMIT');
} catch (error) {
  await client.query('ROLLBACK');
  console.error('Transaction failed:', error);
}
```

Best practices include using connection pooling, securing credentials, validating input to prevent SQL injection, and performing regular database backups to ensure data integrity.

Deploying Bun.js Applications

Preparing Bun.js Applications for Production

Before deploying a Bun.js application to production, ensure your app is optimized and ready. Key steps include:

- **Minifying assets**: Compress JavaScript, CSS, and other static files.
- **Setting production configurations**: Disable debug logs, enable performance optimizations, and set production mode settings in your configuration files.
- **Security enhancements**: Apply security headers (e.g., CORS, Content Security Policy) and implement HTTPS.

Deploying on Cloud Platforms (e.g., Vercel, AWS, DigitalOcean)

You can deploy Bun.js applications on various cloud platforms with ease:

- **Vercel**: Ideal for small to medium-sized apps, Vercel provides automatic deployments and serverless functions.
  - Simply connect your GitHub repository, and Vercel will handle deployment.
- **AWS (Amazon Web Services)**: For larger, more scalable apps, services like **EC2** or **Elastic Beanstalk** are perfect for hosting Bun.js.
  - Use EC2 for full control or Elastic Beanstalk for managed deployments.
- **DigitalOcean**: Offers simple virtual machines with droplets. It's a cost-effective option for hosting Bun.js by setting up a Linux server, installing Bun, and running your application.

Each platform has a unique process for deploying apps, but Bun.js works efficiently on all.

Managing Environment Variables and Configurations

Properly managing environment variables is crucial to ensure that sensitive information like API keys, database credentials, and secret tokens are protected. Use `.env` files to store environment variables and load them into your Bun.js application.

For example, using **dotenv**:

```
import dotenv from 'dotenv';
dotenv.config();

// Accessing an environment variable
console.log(process.env.API_KEY);
```

Be sure to exclude `.env` files from your version control by adding them to `.gitignore`.

Monitoring and Performance Optimization

Monitoring helps keep track of your app's health and performance. Use tools like **Prometheus** or **Grafana** to monitor metrics like memory usage, CPU load, and response times.

For performance optimization:

- **Use caching**: Implement caching strategies like **Redis** to speed up data retrieval.
- **Load balancing**: Distribute traffic across multiple instances of your Bun.js app to avoid overloading a single server.
- **Minimize database calls**: Optimize database queries to reduce response times.

Additionally, consider using a **Content Delivery Network (CDN)** to serve static assets quickly to users around the world.

Testing and Debugging Bun.js Applications

Writing Unit and Integration Tests

Testing is essential for maintaining the quality of your Bun.js applications. Unit tests focus on individual components or functions, while integration tests ensure that different parts of your application work together.

For unit testing, you can write tests for small, isolated pieces of logic, like a function or a route handler:

```
import { assertEquals } from "bun:test";

function add(a, b) {
  return a + b;
}

test("add function", () => {
  assertEquals(add(2, 3), 5);
});
```

Integration tests verify interactions between components, such as testing an API endpoint that communicates with a database.

```
test("GET /users should return all users",
async () => {
```

```
  const res = await fetch("/users");
  const data = await res.json();
  assertEquals(res.status, 200);
  assert(Array.isArray(data));
});
```

Using Bun.js Testing Tools (e.g., Bun's Built-in Test Runner)

Bun.js comes with a built-in test runner that makes writing and running tests simple and efficient. To use it, place your test cases inside a file with a `.test.ts` or `.test.js` extension, and Bun will automatically detect and run them.

Run tests using:

```
bun test
```

The test runner offers features like assertions (`assertEquals`, `assertThrows`) and async test support, making it a versatile tool for testing Bun.js applications.

Debugging Techniques and Tools for Bun.js

When debugging Bun.js applications, you can rely on various techniques and tools to troubleshoot effectively:

- **Console logs**: Using `console.log()` is a quick way to check values at runtime.

- **Bun's debugger**: Bun integrates with Node.js-compatible debuggers, so you can use tools like **VSCode's debugger** or **Chrome DevTools**.

   You can launch Bun.js in debug mode with:

   ```
   bun --inspect index.ts
   ```

- **Error handling**: Catching errors with `try-catch` blocks or using error-handling middleware ensures that exceptions are handled gracefully.

For more complex bugs, you can set breakpoints and step through your code in a debugger to find issues.

Ensuring Performance with Load Testing

Load testing helps ensure that your Bun.js application can handle high traffic and stress conditions. Tools like **k6** or **Apache JMeter** can simulate large numbers of requests to your application and measure performance metrics like latency and error rates.

Here's an example of a simple load test using **k6**:

```
import http from 'k6/http';
import { check, sleep } from 'k6';

export let options = {
  vus: 100,   // Number of virtual users
  duration: '30s',  // Test duration
};

export default function () {
  let res = http.get('http://localhost:3000/users');
  check(res, {
    'status is 200': (r) => r.status === 200,
  });
  sleep(1);
}
```

Running load tests helps you identify performance bottlenecks, enabling you to optimize your app for real-world usage.

Conclusion and Next Steps

Recap of Key Bun.js Concepts

In this book, we explored the core features and practical applications of Bun.js, from setting up projects to building APIs, working with databases, and deploying scalable applications. We covered:

- **TypeScript integration** for safe and maintainable code.
- **Creating and managing HTTP servers** with efficient routing.
- **Building RESTful APIs** and handling real-time communication using WebSockets.
- **Microservices architecture** and database integration for modern backend development.
- **Testing, debugging**, and optimizing performance for production readiness.

Bun.js is a versatile, high-performance runtime that simplifies backend development while maintaining compatibility with the JavaScript ecosystem.

Best Practices for Bun.js Development

To build reliable and scalable Bun.js applications, keep these best practices in mind:

- **Keep code modular**: Structure your code into reusable components and services.
- **Optimize performance**: Use caching, efficient database queries, and load balancing to ensure your application performs well under load.
- **Secure your application**: Implement proper authentication (JWT, OAuth), handle sensitive data with environment variables, and protect against common vulnerabilities like SQL injection.
- **Write tests**: Ensure the quality of your code with unit, integration, and load testing to catch issues early and improve maintainability.

Resources for Continued Learning (Documentation, Communities, Projects)

To continue improving your Bun.js skills, here are some valuable resources:

- **Official Documentation**: The Bun.js documentation (**https://bun.sh/docs**) is a comprehensive resource for learning advanced features, new updates, and best practices.
- **Open-Source Projects**: Explore the Bun.js GitHub repository and other open-source projects to see real-world implementations and contribute to the community.
- **Communities**: Join online communities such as:
    - Bun.js Discord Server
    - Stack Overflow for JavaScript and Bun.js-specific questions
    - GitHub discussions for contributing to Bun.js development

Looking Forward: The Future of Bun.js

Bun.js is rapidly evolving, with new features and performance improvements being introduced regularly. As it grows, you can expect:

- **Improved compatibility** with more JavaScript libraries and frameworks.
- **Enhanced performance** for even faster server-side applications.
- **Broader adoption**, with more developers and companies leveraging Bun.js in production environments.

Staying engaged with the Bun.js community will help you keep up with these developments and continue building cutting-edge applications.

Thank You and Congratulations!

Congratulations on completing *Bun.js in Action: Real-World Solutions for Building Modern Backends*!

We hope this book has helped you on your journey to mastering Bun.js and building fast, scalable backends with modern web technologies. You've learned everything from the basics to advanced techniques, including API development, microservices, real-time communication, and more.

This book was crafted from both the author's experience in the field and with the assistance of AI tools to ensure clarity, structure, and a rich learning experience. We aimed to create a resource that is practical, accessible, and full of real-world examples that you can apply directly to your own projects.

Thank you for choosing this book as part of your learning journey. Your success is our motivation, and we hope to see you use what you've learned to create something incredible!

If this book has been helpful to you, we'd love to hear your feedback! Please consider leaving a review and rating it. Your support helps others discover this resource. And if you think your friends, colleagues, or family members could benefit from this book, feel free to share it with them as well!

For more learning resources and updates, visit: https://9xcode.com/

Happy coding,
Kumar.Abhiii

www.ingramcontent.com/pod-product-compliance
Lightning Source LLC
Chambersburg PA
CBHW070203230526
45471CB00002B/800